Stories for Children with
Problems and Wishes
A Therapeutic Workbook for Turning Problems into Gifts

Text—

Burt G. Wasserman

Artwork and Layout—

William R. Coughlan

Library of Congress Catalog Card No. 94-70338

Printing (Last Digit)

9   8   7   6   5   4   3   2   1

Publisher—

Educational Media Corporation®
PO Box 21311
Minneapolis, MN55421-0311

(612) 781-0088

For Educational Media Corporation—

Production editor—

Don L. Sorenson

Graphic Design—

Earl R. Sorenson

Preface

The text of this therapeutic workbook has been written by a Licensed Professional Counselor who specializes in working with children. The goal is for children to see their problems from a different perspective. When children can look at their problems differently, they become more open to making necessary changes.

Children need to appreciate themselves for their ability to change, so future problems become opportunities to learn, and angry and sad feelings become signals to talk to somebody who can help them change the way they feel.

We invite you to read these vignettes with your children, so you may help them learn the art of changing problems into gifts. Because this material alludes to serious concerns that some children may have, there is a possibility that your child may react with intense feelings as a result of reading a particular therapeutic vignette. If this happens, please do not be alarmed; instead, understand that the cartoon may have helped your child identify a problem that may need the attention of a professional counselor.

This workbook was created to be used by helping professionals, loving parents and guardians, and concerned others. These special adults will be referred to collectively as *guides*. The goals of the workbook are to help children cope with problems, adjust to change, and to learn how to make changes in their own lives.

This workbook is for all children with wishes. Children with wishes want things to change. The title was chosen so the guide can introduce the workbook by asking the child, "Do you have any wishes?"

Most children will have at least one wish that they can share with their guide. This will make for a smooth transition into the workbook. It will also set up for the child the format of talking about one's own feelings as the cartoon vignettes are read and discussed.

This workbook is also for children who *don't* have any wishes. When children don't even have any wishes, it may be a reflection of the helplessness and powerlessness they feel. These children may benefit from using this book with a licensed professional counselor. When this workbook is used with a counselor or other helping professional, the special needs of these children can be evaluated.

The suggestions for drawing are to help stimulate children to get in touch with their feelings. Drawings may also act as a supplement to the questions of the guide. For example, a child who doesn't have any wishes may respond to the directive to "draw things the way you would like them to be."

Please have extra paper, pencil, and markers so the child gets used to the idea of drawing to get in touch with feelings.

Table of Contents

Part 1

Turning Problems into Gifts

Children have always had problems…

In Biblical times, Eliazer, the son of Moses, might have worried about living up to the Ten Commandments that God gave to his father.

In the days of Robin Hood, children sometimes wondered… was robbing from the rich to give to the poor really okay?

In the days of the Old West, being the fastest 10-year-old with a gun was a problem. It meant there was someone waiting out there for you to grow up so he could show you that he was faster than you.

Once, a boy found a very famous art treasure. It was a sculpture which was very valuable but stayed on the ocean floor for a thousand years because it had landed upside down, and no one could see what it really was. It wasn't until the boy—who was diving for pearls—got stuck on a piece of the sculpture that he was forced to look at this thing from all sides and from every angle in order to get himself untangled and free.

It was at that time that he discovered that underneath every problem there are also hidden gifts.

The gifts can only be found by those who look at their problems in many different ways.

Taking Control of Your Problems

1) Did you ever feel very sad because of a problem you had?

2) Are you still sad about that problem or were you able to make the problem a little better?

3) What did you do to make the problem a little better?

4) Do you already know a little bit about changing problems so they don't hurt so much?

Could you draw a picture showing what **you did** (or could do) to change a problem from hurting so much?

Brenda thinks it's a problem that she has to spend so much time on her homework…

But when she puts her "magic future glasses" on… she can see that studying has surely…

…paid off.

Not having much spending money because he has to save for his mom's birthday present is sure a problem for Jamal now…

But when he looks at his problem from another direction —the future—he realizes that whatever he gets his mom…

…will really make his mom happy and that he will feel good inside too!

Looking into the Future

1) Do you ever remember a time when you were worried about something and you never thought it would get any better?

2) What was it that you were worried about?

3) Did that problem go away or at least get a little better?

4) What would it be like if you had "magic future glasses?" What problem would you be able to see differently?

Draw a picture of yourself in the future without having that problem anymore.

Sue Ling's problem was that she was very sad. Her grandmother had died and all she could think of was how much she missed her.

It wasn't until her grandfather talked to her that she learned...

...that thinking of how lucky she was to have such a wonderful grandmother made it a little easier...

...because she knew a part of her grandmother —her memories— would always be with her.

Running Cub was a little Indian boy who had a problem. He was sad because the color of his skin was not the same as all his friends and he felt very different.

It wasn't until his father spoke to him about his great-great-grandfather Running Bear that he felt a tremendous amount of pride in his Native American heritage.

How many of his friends had an Indian Chief as a great-great-grandfather?

Pleasant Memories

1) Have you ever had a pet that died?

2) Have you known any people who have died?

3) What pleasant memories do you keep with you so you can always have that warm feeling in your heart?

4) Do you get sad when you realize that some people treat other people differently, just because of the color of their skin?

Would you like to draw a picture about a pleasant memory of a pet or a person who has died?
Or would you like to draw a picture of a world where everybody feels equal and can live happily together?

Sarah had a very, very big problem. Her parents had separated and had recently decided to get a divorce.

She would often get sad when she thought of them fighting and her being alone.

As she talked to her counselor about it, she began to realize that the problem of the divorce had actually turned into many gifts:

She was able to spend more quality time with both of her parents...

...she was able to meet a whole new bunch of friends...

...who lived in the new neighborhood where her dad's house was...

...and most important of all, her parents weren't fighting anymore and everybody was a lot happier.

So sometimes problems that seem really awful at first work out for the best after a little time goes by.

Things Will Get Better

1) Many children have experienced the divorce of their parents. If you have, you are not alone.

2) When parents separate, the bad feeling children get lasts a long time. This is a situation where it takes a longer time for the other side of the divorce, the positive side, to surface.

3) Just as there are two sides to a coin, there are two sides to a divorce: the painful side and the more peaceful side.

4) If you are experiencing a divorce, try to remember that there will be better times for you in the future. You won't always feel this bad.

If you are experiencing a divorce, put your magic glasses on so you can draw the better times of the future.
You may also use this space to draw a picture of you doing something with your family.

Helen was always very sad. Her father was an alcoholic and she couldn't get him to stop drinking.

She felt nobody had a problem like she did. It wasn't until she went to an Al-A-Teen meeting that she found out that there were many teens that shared the same problem... and some were even her friends.

She also found out that it was not her job to get her father to stop drinking...

AL-A-TEEN

...and that she could learn to feel better about her life by just enjoying being a kid.

Freddy's big problem was that he got caught stealing a water pistol from the store.

He was pretty sad and embarrassed when he got caught, especially since it was the first time he tried to steal anything

It wasn't until he learned about the consequences of stealing that he realized how lucky he was to get caught the first time he tried. Then he started to think about his older brother Mark, who never got caught when he was younger but is in jail now for stealing a television.

Problems to Gifts

1) Have you ever worried about your father because he drinks or your mom because there never seems to be enough money to pay the bills?

2) Those are adult problems, and like Helen, all children should have a chance to play and just be a kid. If you are worrying about something you can't control, talk about it to the person who is helping you read this book.

3) Have you ever wanted to steal something? Have you ever stolen something and not been caught?

4) Can you understand why Freddy was lucky he got caught?

Can you draw a picture of how you might change the problem you have into a gift?

Mary felt strange when her stepfather would play with her. She had an "icky" feeling that something was not right.

Her problem was that she was afraid to talk to her mom about the feeling because she knew how much her mom loved her husband. She was also afraid her mom wouldn't believe her.

When she talked to her counselor, she assured Mary that her mother would like to know.

Mary talked to her mother, and her stepfather went to a counselor to learn the difference between good touching and bad touching.

Johnny was very confused about his problem. His best friend Sam always talked about his own private parts, but now he wanted to play with Johnny's. He even said he wouldn't be his best friend anymore if Johnny didn't play "the touching game."

Like may little boys, Johnny liked to look at his own private parts and compare it with his friends… but touching was another thing… that's why they call it private! But he didn't want to lose his friend.

He told his mom and she told him to say NO!

He did and he and Sam are still friends.

Sam is also going to a counselor to learn more about his problem with touching.

12

Listening to Your Inner Voice

1) The important thing to remember is that you should always listen to that voice inside that tells you when something doesn't feel right ("icky feeling").

2) Many children are approached by other children, adults and even relatives who feel it's okay to touch a child's private parts. *It's NOT okay and you MUST TELL SOMEONE!*

3) Has anything ever happened to you that caused you to hear that voice inside telling you to *TELL SOMEONE?*

4) Sometimes that voice tells you not to do other things, like not to steal a piece of candy, or not to go into your mother's pocketbook, or not to be cruel to the new kid on the block. People call that voice their *conscience.*

Can you draw a picture that tells a story about a time
you remember hearing that voice inside tell you something important?

Summary

All these stories are about children who all had something in common. Let's look back and see. There was Jamal who worried, Brenda who didn't have confidence that she was doing the right thing, Sue Ling who was sad about her loss, Running Cub who felt different, Sarah and Helen who were sad, Freddy who was embarrassed, and Mary and Johnny who were confused. What did all these children have in common?

They all had problems.

They all had uncomfortable feelings that went with their problems. (That's why they call them problems.)

They all used those uncomfortable feelings as **signals to do something**.

And most important of all, they all were able to **change their problems.**

Jamal and Brenda were able to change the way they looked at their problems by pretending to step out of the present and into the future so that they could see the way things would be in a few days or a whole bunch of years. Sometimes children are so sad because their problems appear so big that they want to end their lives. They say things like, "I wish I were dead." Those children need to remember that **things will change and they won't always feel so bad.**

Sue Ling still missed her grandmother, but instead of staying sad when she thought of her, the pleasant memories of the past made her feel warm inside.

Running Cub was sad about being different until he thought about it in another way. It was then that he realized **being different means you are special.**

It is difficult when your parents separate and get a divorce. In some ways, thinking about it will hurt Sarah for a long time. But Sarah learned to also think of the other side of her problem, the good side. Sometimes it takes a while for children and adults to be able to see the other side of a problem.

The next time you have a problem you can be curious to see: "How long will it take me to see the other side of my problem?"

Freddy learned that the other side of his problem was that he could stop stealing before it turned into a habit.

Helen learned that her father's drinking **was not her problem.**

Children shouldn't worry about problems they can't control. They also need to remember that if they are being touched in their private parts, being yelled at all the time or being beaten, they need to **TELL SOMEONE**, so they can be in control.

So remember these things about problems:

All problems offer opportunities to learn

Problems are like mistakes:
the more mistakes you make—or the more problems
you have—the more you learn

We can all learn to see our problems differently

When we can see our problems differently,
we can also see new solutions

and most important of all,

Always appreciate yourself when you take time
to learn about yourself.

Part 2

Turning Wishes into Goals

Wishes without Feet

1. What do you think a wish without feet is?

2. It is a wish that you have no control over, and whatever you do or however hard you wish, it will only come true if **other people** do something differently.

3. It's like wishing for snow on Christmas. You can't control that wish by doing anything differently.

4. A wish that has feet is one that can happen if **you** do something differently. For example, a wish to get a better grade in math class would be a wish with feet because you could do something differently: study harder.

5. A wish with no feet is one that only happens if **someone else** does something differently. For example, "I wish Mom and Dad would get back together." Children have no control about getting their parents back together; it's something their parents have to do. Their parents didn't separate because of their children, and as hard as children try, **they** can't get their parents back together.

My Wishes

A Wish with Feet   A Wish with No Feet

You need to have a **plan**. When you have a plan, you will be able to turn a wish into a goal. The best plan is one that is **clear, positive, realistic** and one that **you** can **control**.

Turning Wishes into Goals

1) A goal is like a wish with feet. It is something you are willing to work hard to achieve.

2) In order to achieve your goal, you need to have a plan; your goal has to be realistic and it must be in your control.

3) There are short-term goals that you want to achieve in the near future, and there are long-term goals that will take years to accomplish.

4) Can you identify any short-term goals that you have already accomplished? Are there any on which you would like to begin to work?

Draw a picture of yourself achieving a short-term goal.

Angry Wishes

1. Sometimes children say things they really don't mean when they are angry. Like, "I wish she were dead." But no matter how angry you are at someone, you can't make a wish come true.

2. Some children feel guilty about their angry wishes and other children are afraid that their wishes might come true.

3. It's normal to have angry thoughts and angry feelings. They are signals that your own feelings have been hurt.

4. The next time you have angry thoughts or feelings, find someone to talk to about how your own feelings have been hurt.

Goal Setting

1) The words we use to state our goals will determine if we achieve our goals.

2) The words we use make pictures in our minds. If our picture is clear, positive and realistic, we are more likely to reach our goal. If the picture is not clear, we will probably just continue to daydream without actually doing anything about it.

3) A clear picture is one where you can see yourself doing the first steps to achieve your goal.

4) The first step to getting a good grade is to study. The first step to developing a good jump shot is to practice. The first step in getting along better with a parent is to make a small change in your behavior.

Draw the first step of yourself achieving a goal.

Goal: "I will treat my brother nicely."

Think before I say anything

Don't tease him

Find something nice
to say to him

Appreciate myself
for changing a bad behavior

Step 1

Step 2

Step 3

Final Goal

If this was your problem, what picture would you draw in each box?

Making Your Own Movie

1) Most children have some type of movie or picture in their heads about how they think they should act.

2) Some children have "macho" movies where they see themselves as acting as tough guys. Other children have "chameleon" movies where they see themselves acting like their friends do in order to fit in.

3) Those children are acting out movies that other people have made for them.

4) When you are in charge of making your own movie, you can make movies to help you achieve a goal that is best for you.

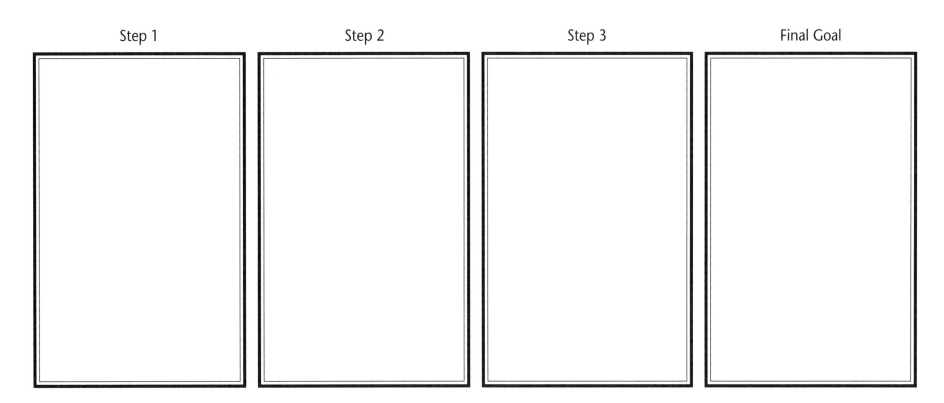

Step 1	Step 2	Step 3	Final Goal

Starting with a picture of your final goal,
draw the other steps or things that need to happen so you can achieve your goal.

Some problems are easy to see differently and turn into gifts.

With other problems, we need time to go by before we realize that things have worked out for the best.

Changing Problems

1) How do you change your problems into gifts?

2) Do you **turn** your problems around?

3) Do you **see** your problems differently?

4) Do you work on your problem until the problem **feels** different?

5) Do you **listen** to solutions until one **sounds** right?

Draw a picture showing how you change your problems into gifts.

For the Guide

LEARNING WITH OUR SENSES

The way children answer the questions on the preceding page may tell you something about their representational system. Do they have a dominant representational system that only allows them to learn when it *feels right*, when they can *see things* differently or if it *sounds fine* to them?

The most efficient learning takes place when people can use all three systems equally: the visual (seeing), the auditory (hearing) and the kinesthetic (feeling). Listen to the words children use to describe things and to communicate that they understand. Do their styles match yours? Or are you speaking in a language they doesn't understand?

Children who have difficulty with one or two of the representational systems and strongly favor the third may experience problems with learning in school and understanding cause-and-effect relationships. A child's ability to visualize is essential as an aid to long-term memory, retrieval of information, and goal achievement.

As you continue to work with a child, be curious to see if a pattern of learning becomes clear. If it does, you will be in a better position to describe things and present material in a way that best meets the child's learning style. Children who have difficulty visualizing may also have difficulty learning in school. When we provide opportunities for children to practice visualization, we can help them strengthen what may be a weak link in their learning strategy. When you speak in the child's language, you are in rapport with the child on a subliminal level. This will increase your flexibility as a communicator and the child's ability to perceive what you are saying. If you begin to notice that the child favors one representational system and ignores another, you now are in a position to help that child become more flexible. When children become aware of the different ways they can learn, they can improve academic performance at school and change problem behaviors at home. With your help they can begin to realize that they don't always have to think and act in their old ways. This becomes the first step in the process of taking responsibility for their own behavior.

Taking Responsibility

1. You are responsible for your own behavior. No one can make you do something or **make you angry**.

2. As a young child, if someone took your toy, you would get angry. As you get older, you will realize that becoming angry is a matter of choice and is something you can control.

3. At times, it is appropriate to get angry. As you get older, you will learn to use the feeling of anger as a signal to make some kind of change.

4. It is okay to be angry. As you get older, you can learn to express your anger in the correct way.

5. When things happen, children often blame their behavior on the thing that "got them angry."

6. Taking responsibility is understanding that it is not what happens but how we perceive (see, hear, feel) what happens that causes us to get upset. **We make ourselves** upset by what we say to ourselves, the pictures we see in our minds, and the things we remember that other people have said.

Understanding Your Behavior

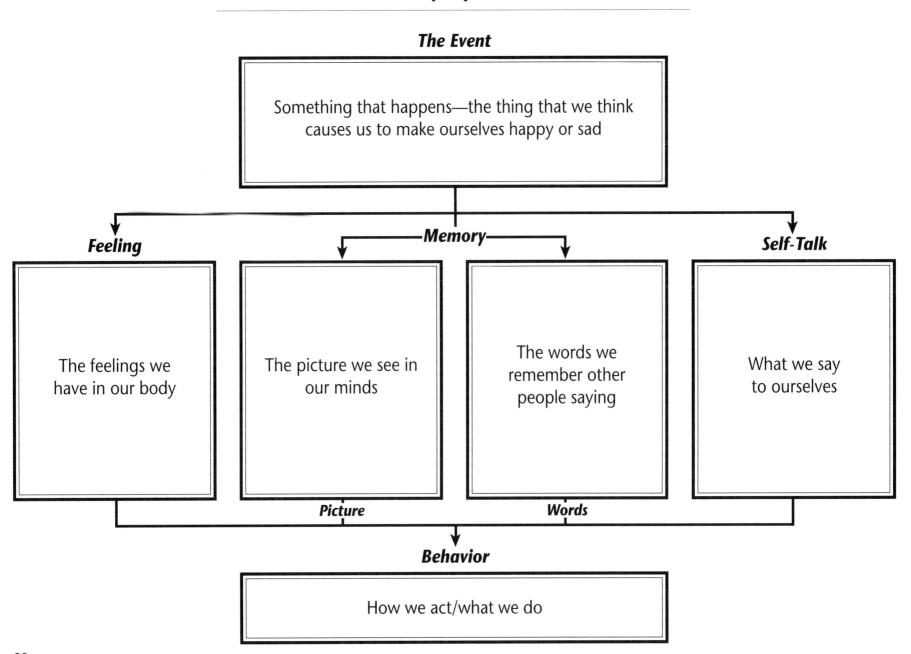

The Event

Something that happens—the thing that we think
causes us to make ourselves happy or sad

Feeling

Memory

Self-Talk

The feelings we
have in our body

The picture we see in
our minds

The words we
remember other
people saying

What we say
to ourselves

Picture

Words

Behavior

How we act/what we do

How We Make Ourselves Angry

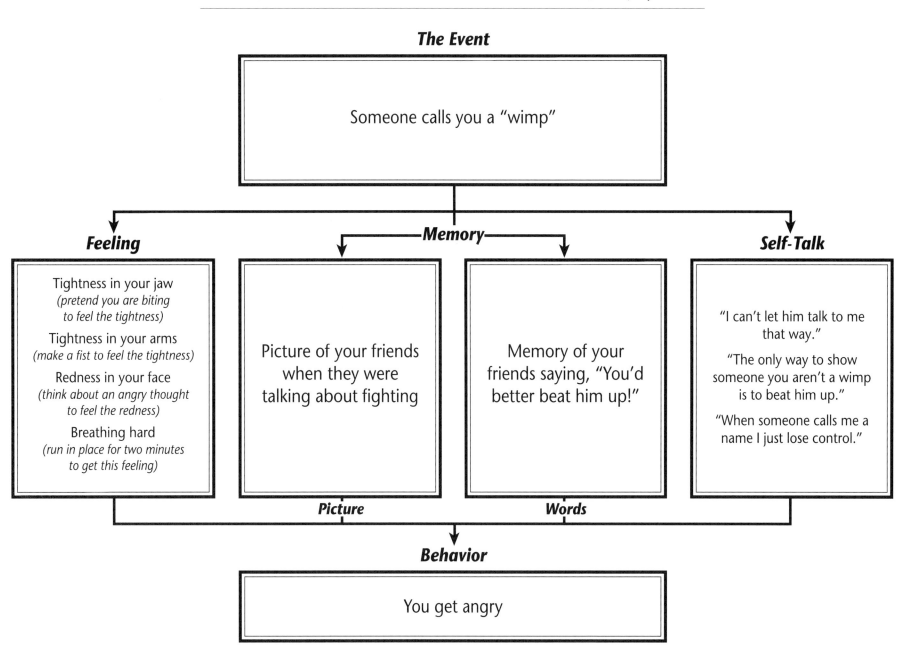

The Event

Someone calls you a "wimp"

Feeling

Tightness in your jaw
(pretend you are biting to feel the tightness)

Tightness in your arms
(make a fist to feel the tightness)

Redness in your face
(think about an angry thought to feel the redness)

Breathing hard
(run in place for two minutes to get this feeling)

Memory

Picture of your friends when they were talking about fighting

Memory of your friends saying, "You'd better beat him up!"

Self-Talk

"I can't let him talk to me that way."

"The only way to show someone you aren't a wimp is to beat him up."

"When someone calls me a name I just lose control."

Picture   *Words*

Behavior

You get angry

Remember, it is not the event or the thing that happens that causes us to lose our tempers. It is what we say to ourselves, what we remember other people saying and the pictures we make in our minds that are the real causes of losing our tempers.

If getting angry is a choice we make, then if we learn to say different things to ourselves and remember different pictures, we can coach ourselves to deal with things without losing our tempers.

What Happens When We Take Responsibility

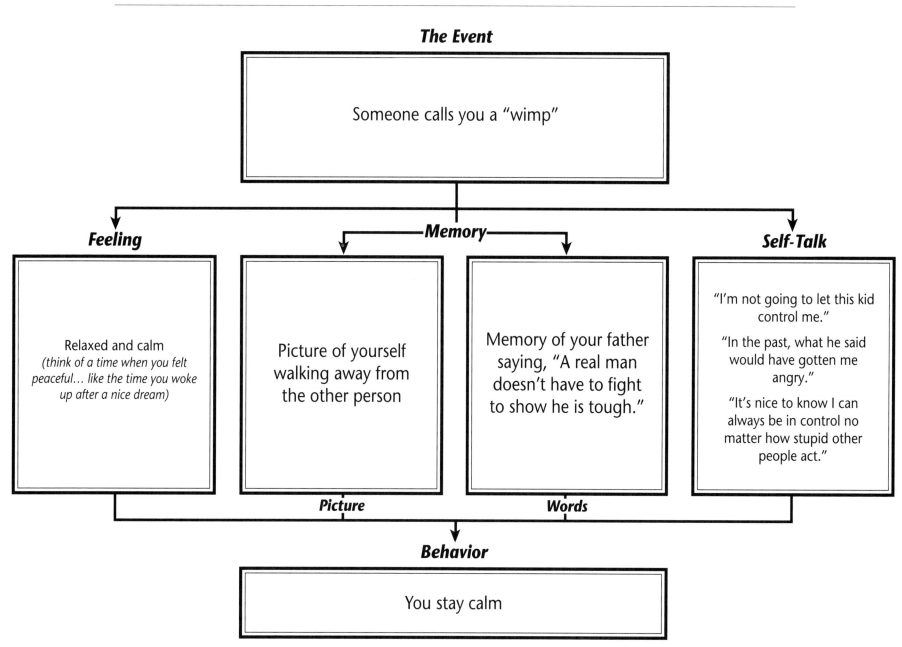

The Event

Someone calls you a "wimp"

Feeling

Memory

Self-Talk

Relaxed and calm
(think of a time when you felt peaceful… like the time you woke up after a nice dream)

Picture of yourself walking away from the other person

Memory of your father saying, "A real man doesn't have to fight to show he is tough."

"I'm not going to let this kid control me."

"In the past, what he said would have gotten me angry."

"It's nice to know I can always be in control no matter how stupid other people act."

Picture

Words

Behavior

You stay calm

1. Can you remember a time when **you thought** someone "made" you angry?

2. Can you remember the things you said to yourself about that person to cause yourself to be angry? How about the picture you had in your mind?

3. What different things could you say to yourself on the next occasion so that you won't lose your temper?

Use the blank flow charts on the next two pages in the future, when you have a behavior you would like to change (you can make copies of the pages if you want). Use the "Negative Behavior" page to illustrate the behavior you want to change, and use the "Solution Behavior" page to illustrate the positive behavior you would like to have.

Understanding Your Behavior

The Event   **Negative Behavior**

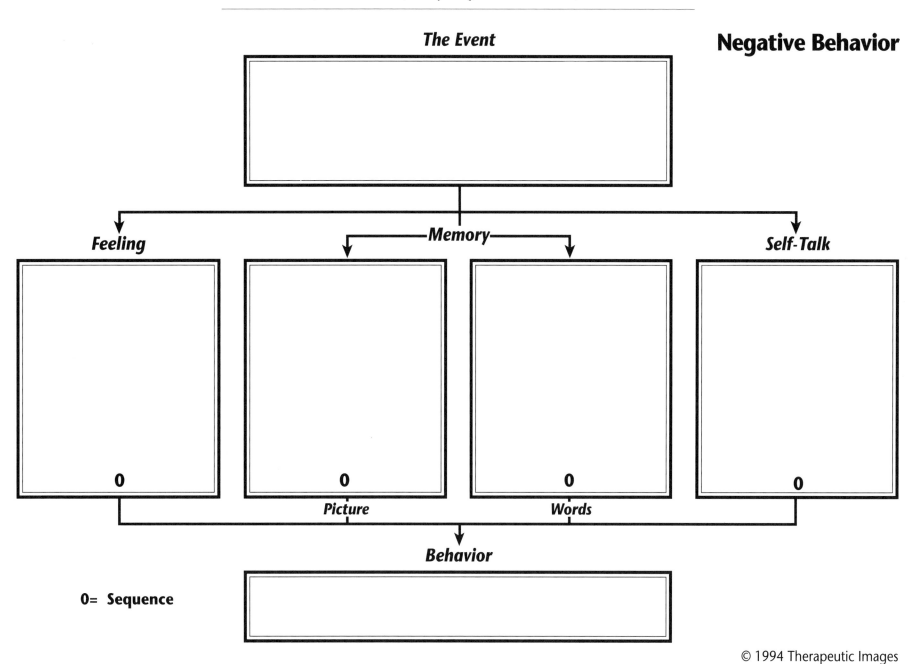

Feeling   *Memory*   *Self-Talk*

0= **Sequence**

0   **0**   **0**   **0**

Picture   *Words*

Behavior

© 1994 Therapeutic Images

Understanding Your Behavior

The Event

Solution Behavior

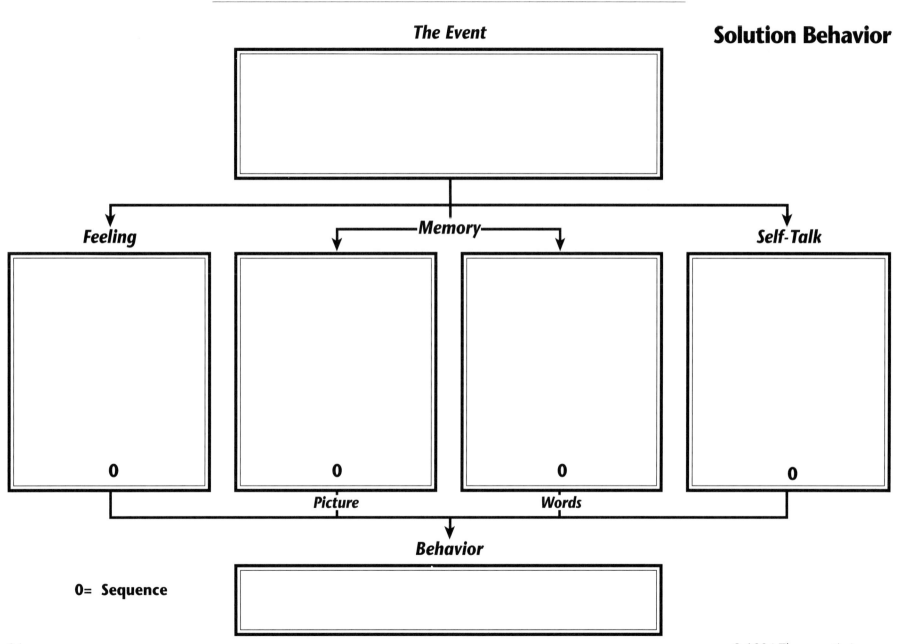

Feeling

Memory

Self-Talk

0

0

0

0

Picture

Words

Behavior

0= Sequence

Your Good Feeling

How does your body experience your good feeling?

Is it:

Tingly or Numb?

Full or Empty?

Light or Heavy?

Relaxed or Tense?

Like an Open Flower or Like a Closed Flower?

High in Your Chest or Low in Your Chest?

If your good feeling had a color, what color would it be?

Are there other ways your body experiences your good feeling?

If you can remember how your body feels when you are happy you can bring that feeling back when you begin to feel uncomfortable about something else.

If you can do that, you have begun to understand a very special way of changing behavior called NLP :

Neuro-Linguistic Programming

Appreciate Yourself

1) It is important to try your best and to always try to improve.

2) But it is equally important to know what you like about yourself so that when times get rough you can still be happy inside.

3) Tell the person that is reading this book with you what you like about yourself. If this is hard for you to do, your friend can help. You can also think about what other people might say about you.

Draw a happy picture of yourself and remember the feeling that goes with the picture.

Anchor It

There are many things in this workbook that are important to remember.

People who study how children learn have found that if you can attach something in your mind—like a picture, a few words or a feeling—to something you want to remember, you are more likely to remember that thing. You will have made your own "mental anchor."

For example, if you want to remember that all problems can be turned around into gifts, you might make a picture in your head of the last problem you changed into a gift.

or

You might remember some words that will get you through the next problem, like, "I got through the last problem—I can get through this one."

or

You might remember the feeling you had when you were able to look at that problem differently.

On the next pages are things that you may want to remember.

Choose the best picture, words and feeling to attach to each thing you want to remember.

Learning Strategy

1. Read the statement at the bottom of each page. Discuss the meaning with the person who is helping you read this book.

2. Make a picture in your mind about your life that will allow you to remember the statement at the bottom of the next page.

3. The more detail you put into the picture in your mind, the better you will be able to remember the statement. Hint: Sometimes very silly pictures become easier to remember.

4. Once you have a good feeling to go along with the picture in your mind, draw that picture on the next page.

5. Choose words that will help you bring back the picture and the feeling that goes with the thing you want to remember. That's called **anchoring it**.

6. Describe the feeling you get when you remember the statement.

7. What part of your body experiences the feeling most?

"I Am In Control of What I Do."

Feelings _____   Words _____

_____   _____

_____   _____

_____   _____

Learning Strategy — Short Form

1. Read and discuss the statement.

2. Make a picture in your mind.

3. Give the picture detail and make it memorable.

4. Draw the picture.

5. Choose words to anchor it.

6. Describe the feeling.

"Every Goal Has a First Step."

Feelings _____

_____

_____

Words _____

_____

_____

Learning Strategy — Short Form

1. Read and discuss the statement.

2. Make a picture in your mind.

3. Give the picture detail and make it memorable.

4. Draw the picture.

5. Choose words to anchor it.

6. Describe the feeling.

"Pictures Help Me Learn."

Feelings _____   Words _____

_____   _____

_____   _____

_____   _____

Learning Strategy — Short Form

1. Read and discuss the statement.

2. Make a picture in your mind.

3. Give the picture detail and make it memorable.

4. Draw the picture.

5. Choose words to anchor it.

6. Describe the feeling.

"I Am Special."

Feelings _____   Words _____

_____   _____

_____   _____

_____

You Are Not Your Behavior

Step 1

Step 2

a) When children behave badly, sometimes they think they are bad people; they feel bad all over.

b) Pick a color that matches the bad feeling you have when you think you are a bad person.

c) Color the picture above with the amount of bad feelings you have.

a) Since *you* are not your *behavior*, and your behavior is something that can be *temporary* and that you can change...

b) Place the color that matches the behavior that you want to change in the balloon.

You Are Not Your Behavior

Step 3

a) The next time you feel filled with the bad behavior feeling, remember to put that feeling into the balloon, so that your behavior can change.

b) If you still feel the bad behavior feelings, you can snap your fingers and wait until this feeling is in the balloon.

Step 4

a) When they are in the balloon, *open your hand* and let go of the balloon.

b) Watch the old behavior float away and notice the new feeling that enters your body.

c) Pick a color to match this new *good behavior feeling* and color the person above with that feeling.

I Am Not My Behavior: My Own Pictures

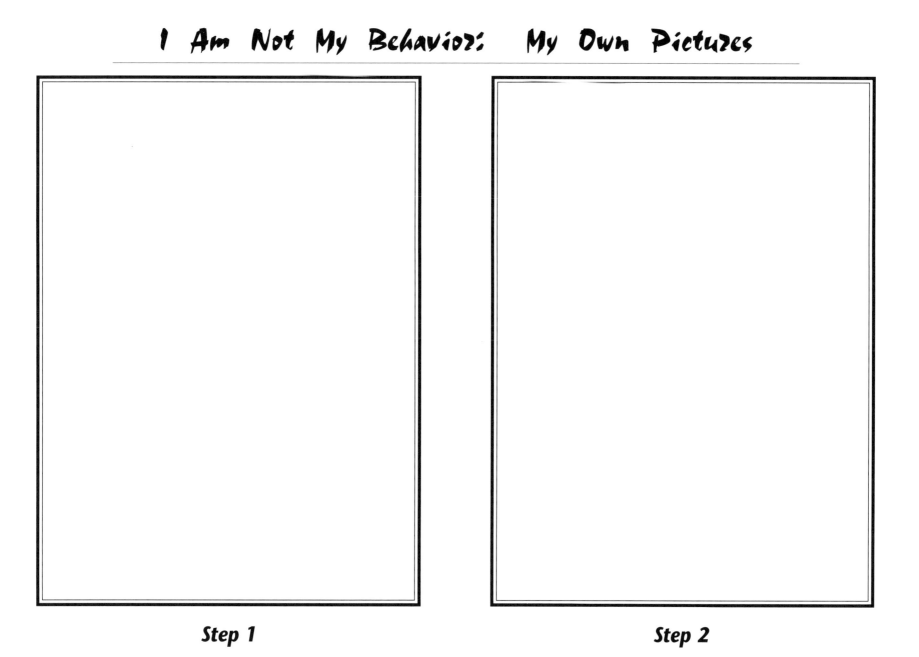

Step 1

Step 2

The next time you have a behavior you would like to change, you can draw your own pictures here.

50

I Am Not My Behavior: My Own Pictures

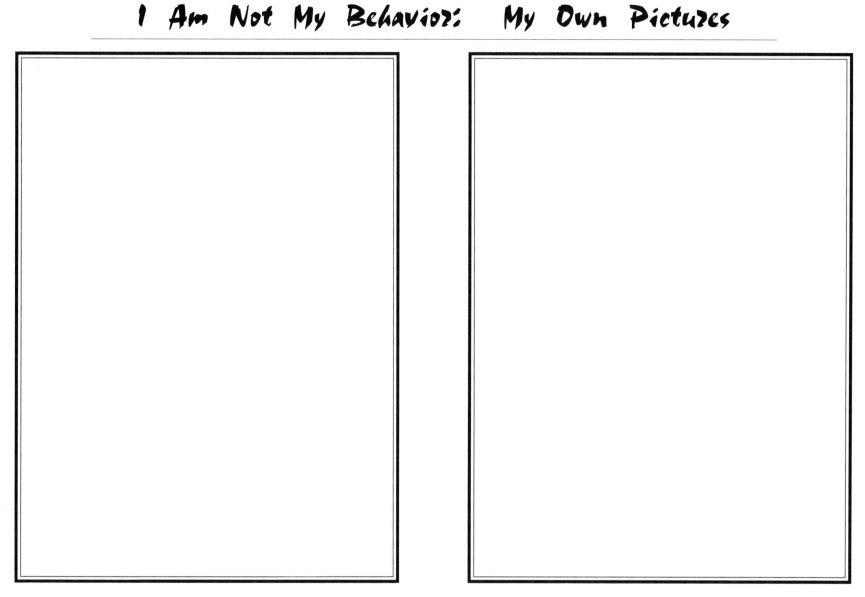

Step 3

Step 4

If the bad behavior comes back, you can remember the pictures you have drawn or colored
and imagine the bad behavior floating away in your imaginary balloon.

Letting Go of Feelings

Step 1

Step 2

a) Pick the color that matches the feeling that you had *at the time when the problem happened.*

b) Color the picture above with as much of the feeling as you had in your body *at the time when the problem happened.*

a) The purpose of counseling is to get the uncomfortable feelings of the past *out of your body.*

b) If there are still even traces of that feeling that you had in the past when you think of the past, put the color of those feelings in the balloon.

Letting Go of Feelings

Step 3

The next time those feelings come back, *snap your fingers* and wait until they are all in the balloon.

Step 4

a) When they are in the balloon, *open your hand* and let go of the balloon.

b) Imagine watching the balloon disappear into the clouds and *notice how your body changes and that you become more relaxed.*

c) Pick a color to match this relaxed feeling and color the person above with that feeling.

Letting Go of My Feelings: My Own Pictures

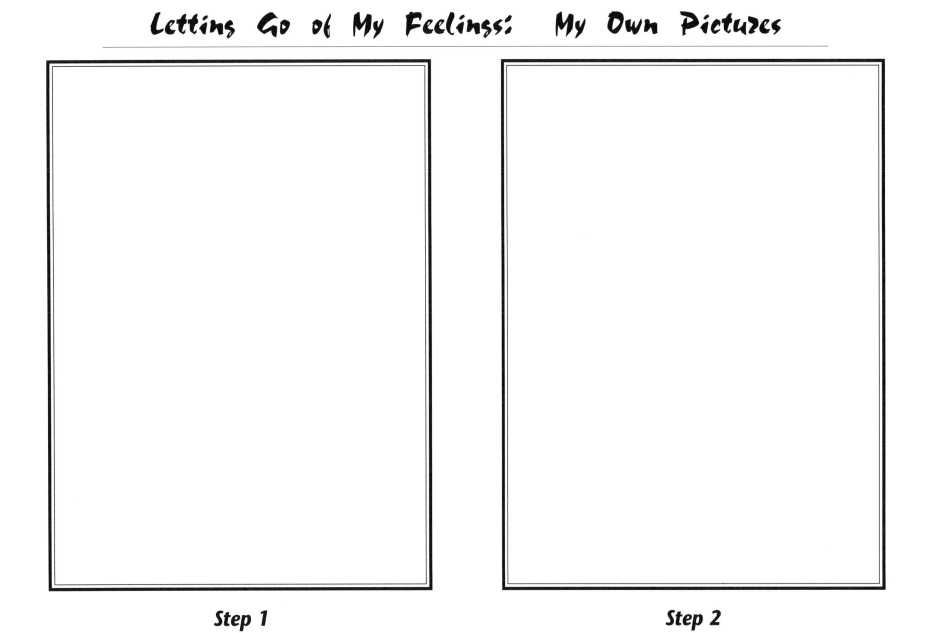

Step 1

Step 2

The next time you have a behavior you would like to change, you can draw your own pictures here.

Letting Go of My Feelings: My Own Pictures

Step 3   **Step 4**

If the bad behavior comes back, you can remember the pictures you have drawn or colored
and imagine the bad behavior floating away in your imaginary balloon.

Thinking about Your Timeline

If the circle marks what you are thinking about in the *present* and the star marks what you will be thinking about in the *future*, are there any memories in the *past* that you don't want to think about in the same way in the *present* or in the *future*?

☐ ————————————————— ○ ————————————————— ☆

Past   Present   Future

Draw a picture of all the feelings of the *past*… so you can leave those feelings on the paper.
If you like, when you are done with your picture, place *bars* over the picture to make sure the feelings can't get out.

The Things I Like about Myself

1. _____

_____

2. _____

_____

3. _____

_____

4. _____

_____

5. _____

_____

6. _____

_____

7. _____

_____

8. _____

_____

9. _____

_____

10. _____

_____

Finding Solutions

There are many ways to find solutions and make changes. The pages that follow will allow you to draw the different strategies you have used to make changes. After you make these final drawings, you can compare them with the first drawings you made in this book. Do you notice how they are different? They are different because you are different. Congratulations, you have learned how to make changes. May your life be filled with positive changes.

A. Seeing Things Differently

B. Going To The Future

Draw your problem picture in a way so you can see things differently. Make the good things about the problem appear bigger so you can remember them.

When you have a picture of what you want things to be like in the future, it makes it easier to get there. Some people say, "If I can see it, I can be it." Draw a picture of the way things will be for you in the future.

C. Looking Back From The Future

Sometimes when we see ourselves in the future, after our problem is solved, we are able to look back and find some solutions to the problems we have in the present. After you take the time you need to see yourself in the future, draw the picture that comes to your mind that will move you toward a solution to your present problem.

D. Listening To Your Inner Voice

Your inner voice always has something to tell you if you take the time to stop and listen. Take the time you need to listen to your inner voice. Draw a picture about what it has told you.

E. Choosing Your Helper

F. Your Special Strengths

QUALITIES:

Self-Control	Patience	Confidence
Peacefulness	Competence	Inner Strength

In the past, special people like a family member, guardian, teacher, coach, religious leader, or close friend, have probably told you something that you might want to remember as part of the solution to your problem. Draw a picture of yourself doing the thing that the special person told you or would tell you if he or she was here now.

Listed above are some qualities that children often need to have in order to find solutions to their problems. Circle the qualities you will need and draw a picture of yourself with these qualities. Remember when you used some of these qualities to solve other problems in the past.

G. Changing Body Feelings

You have learned that you can change the way you feel as the result of what you say to yourself, what you remember others saying, the pictures you make in your mind, and the qualities that you decide to use. Take a deep breath, release that breath as you close your eyes and imagine what a picture of that good body feeling would be like. Draw that picture.

H. Finding New Meanings to Old Behaviors

When you understand old, unwanted behaviors in new ways, it allows you to let them go. Have you been able to put a different meaning to an old, unwanted behavior? Can you draw a picture about that?

1. Positive Energy

Sometimes solutions happen because of all the good (positive) energy that you and others have used to solve your problem. Good energy is made when you relax and let your mind daydream about all the different ways your problem will be solved. Good energy also is made when your counselor understands you so well that his or her good energy can mix with yours to find a solution or heal a wound. Good energy is also made when you pray to God.

If that good energy had a shape, what shape do you think you would make it? What colors would you use to draw that positive energy? Draw a picture of yourself surrounded by the positive energy that you have created in your search to find solutions to your problem. If you like, you may draw other people in your picture that may benefit from this positive energy in the future.

Great Job!

Give your helper a good handshake.

If your helper is your mom, your dad or someone you love very much… you might want to give your helper a **hug!**

Now get started changing your problems into gifts. And **thanks!**

Burt and Bill

Appendix: More about NLP

This workbook was developed to help children learn to cope with situations in new and different ways. The workbook is based upon the principles of *Neuro-Linguistic Programming* (NLP), which is a methodology that has its roots in General Semantics developed in the 1930s and was co-developed by Richard Bandler and John Grinder in the mid-1970s.

NLP was designed as a result of a systematic study of Milton Erickson, a psychiatrist and hypnotherapist; Virginia Satir, a family therapist; and others who demonstrated excellence in their field. After the co-developers identified the verbal and nonverbal patterns that were effective, they designed a structure for these events and a methodology to duplicate them with other patients and clients.

Since that time a number of brilliant individuals in the therapeutic community who have been trained by Bandler and Grinder have expanded their original work. Foremost among these individuals are Leslie Cameron-Bandler, Michael Grinder, Connirae and Steve Andreas, Robert Dilts and Ron Klein. Each year the methodology of NLP becomes more widely accepted in the therapeutic and educational community. It is my hope that *Problems and Wishes* contributes to that acceptance as well as introduces NLP to parents wishing to interact with their children in effective ways.

The attractiveness of NLP lies in its universal applicability. It is a methodology that can enhance any therapeutic style of intervention, any educational or personal growth goal, as well as the quality of any communication between two or more people. As a result, it could improve the communication between parent and child, husband and wife, teacher and student, and coach and athlete. I am particularly excited about NLP because of its adaptability to the field of Special Education and its suitability in helping children who have been diagnosed as having a learning disability or attention deficit disorder.

Some Basic Principles

Each time I write about NLP I find that I can see it in different ways. That shouldn't surprise me because my whole philosophy of counseling is based upon the premise that my purpose as a counselor is to provide an opportunity for children to see things differently so they can turn their problems into gifts. The term that is used for this phenomenon in the therapeutic community is "reframing."

When we place something in a new frame we begin to see it differently. We no longer have trouble seeing "the forest for the trees" and we can truly understand why "shallow waters run deep." The reframe that I have found to be most helpful came from the work of Erickson and is a presupposition of NLP. It states that, at one time, most behaviors had a positive purpose.

This reframing enables children who misbehave to simply find another way to satisfy their positive intentions. It also enables parents to realize that the behaviors that they want to change as adults may have had some positive origins at one time earlier in life. Many adults from dysfunctional families find it hard to trust and share their feelings with others. This is quite understandable when one views the positive origins of the behavior, which started when they were children in their homes.

Another basic presupposition of NLP focuses on the relationship between flexibility and personal power. The more flexible a child is in terms of being open to see things from different viewpoints, the more personal power or natural resources that child will have.

NLP teaches children to develop strategies to increase their flexibility so they can react to things in positive ways. The beauty of NLP is that children don't have to learn the entire package but only what they need to learn to expand their learning strategies.

NLP is particularly well suited for children with learning disabilities and attention deficit disorder. The activities in this workbook ask children to become aware of how they perceive things. When children work with this modality they sharpen their ability to learn from what they see, hear and feel. Children also learn to intensify their imagery so they can better understand an inappropriate strategy and develop a different strategy for change.

Therapists have been using visual imagery for many years. When they incorporate the principles of NLP, they are able to expand the impact of the imagery by asking children to pay attention to the submodalities of the pictures in their minds. When children are asked to hear the sounds within the picture and smell the smells, the picture often becomes more vivid. The more vivid the picture, the easier it becomes to access other information like the child's self-talk and how the body experiences a particular feeling.

As the workbook has illustrated, by focusing on the submodalities of the children's internal representational system, they can learn how they make bad feelings. By taking responsibility for making their feelings, children take control to change those feelings. When children who are phobic are asked, "How do you do that?" and are told that they are already masters at communicating with their bodies, they are provoked to look at their problems in a different light. It almost appears as if they have a real talent.

The major concept of this workbook is that once children identify how their bodies experience positive feelings, those feelings become "natural resources." Children can use their natural resources from the past in new "problem situations." More important, the feeling state can be transferred content-free. This means that the feeling of confidence that children might have on the playing field can be remembered by the body and brought back in a different context; for example, prior to taking a test. When children do this, they have "anchored" this good feeling and have brought it back when they needed it.

When children "collapse" a positive anchor into a negative problem state, they are performing the most basic procedure in NLP. Children who have been diagnosed as having ADD can, at times, avoid the need to use medication by anchoring positive feeling states in what used to be problem situations. Although I do not choose at this time to make the elimination of medication a goal, I do teach children that are taking medication for ADD to memorize how their body experiences the medication. If people can reduce tumors with imagery, it is reasonable to believe that they can also duplicate the effect of a medication such as Ritalin. The underlying presupposition that the child is still in control is a very important one for someone being treated for ADD, ADHD, or any other behavior or affective disorder.

The most efficient learning, "whole brain learning," is one that can incorporate all three modalities in a learning strategy. Children with learning disabilities usually learn primarily through one or two modalities without using the third. If they are weakest in terms of using their visual representational system, they will have problems with learning in school. When parents and educators use the principles of NLP, children can learn to strengthen weak areas. More advanced NLP procedures are also available for the therapist who is working with children who have experienced traumas, are phobic, or are simply having a difficult time adjusting to a life situation.

Undoubtedly the most exciting aspect of NLP is how quickly people can change using this methodology. In addition to some significant personal changes I have made in my own life using this technology, I have witnessed my clients experience countless changes. Within a forty-minute period I was able to completely eliminate an 18-year-old's phobia for test taking and dramatically reduce her study time by approximately 50%. This was done in one session by teaching her to collapse anchors prior to taking a test and to learn a spelling strategy in which she visualized the word and then read it rather than remembering a mnemonic for each word. Her strategy was not an isolated one, as I learned after reading one of Sid Jacobson's books which described a poor speller who used the phrase, "A rat in Tom's house might eat Tom's ice cream." When I asked my client if she had heard that phrase before, she sat, thought and said, "Oh, that's arithmetic." Obviously she had a highly developed auditory channel which she used to learn to spell. Fortunately, in 20 minutes she was able to learn to visualize words, instead of remembering a mnemonic. That 20 minutes changed her life. She decreased her study time, and more important, she felt better about herself.

Not all my sessions are that dramatic, nor do all the children I work with change immediately. However, each time they come they are working on strategies and solutions. Each time they come they are learning a little bit more about themselves-how they think, how they make feelings and how they learn.

Some Clinical Applications

There is no substitute for good training, supervision, and lots of reading. A good place to start is the bibliography which offers a selection of articles and books that could be most helpful in expanding your understanding of this approach to working with children. In response to a suggestion of a distinguished reviewer, Dr. J.D. Ball, I am offering some other examples of how this methodology has been utilized in a clinical setting.

One of the most useful features of this workbook has been the numerous ways my clients (both children and adults) have used the "Understanding Your Behavior Chart." The complaint I hear most often is that "he made me mad" or "she got me angry." With this chart, children learn that no one can "make them angry." They also learn that they are the ones that make themselves angry by the way they reacted to the other child. Once they realize that they are responsible for working themselves into an angry frenzy, they can begin to make choices and program other strategies into their mind and body to formulate a more appropriate solution behavior.

What is often interesting is how the structure and sequence of their negative behavior differs from their solution behavior. At times, their negative behavior goes from the event straight to the feeling of the behavior. Once they are taught that they can use this self-talk, pictures, and auditory memories of the past, they realize they have other options and, therefore, can be in control of their behavior. The result has been that the chart has been used by children and adolescents to control their temper, to avoid pulling a knife, to stop stealing and lying, and even to deal with the past trauma of being sexually abused. The significance of the chart is that it goes beyond traditional cognitive therapy to include imagery and an awareness of how the body experiences the desired feeling (calmness) and trait (self-control). Even when the problem behavior involves all four components, the sequence of the solution behavior will often change. This results in a pattern interruption which becomes an essential ingredient for change.

The use of art as a therapeutic tool is another important feature of this workbook. The therapist does not have to be trained to interpret children's art to use art as a therapeutic tool. The directions that you give the child to draw include important subliminal presuppositions. They include: "You are in control of your behavior; things will be changing for you over time; and you can draw the ways that you will change."

When children draw, they make the feeling concrete instead of amorphous. Sometimes when it is a nightmare they are drawing, they are asked to put bars over it so the monster can't get off the paper. The wonderful thing about asking children to draw is that you can ask them to draw the same thing you can ask them to visualize in hypnotherapy. *This book allows children to benefit from the structure of hypnotherapy without you ever having to ask them to close their eyes.*

Usually the interventions that focus on the Understanding Behavior Chart become permanent changes. Conversely, some of the physiological shifts that occur from the drawing activity sometimes only last for a few weeks to a few months. This may be more a factor of the age of the children who need to rely on the art activities rather than the cognitive nature of the chart. The important thing is that the art activities provide small break-throughs and set the children up for more permanent changes as they get older.

An important premise of this workbook is that a past success of the child becomes *a personal resource* that child will always have to use to solve other problems in the future. What is not always clear with traditional therapies is how easily a success in one area can be linked to a solution of a problem in another area of the child's life. The key factor is that each of our bodies experienced a past success in a unique way. NLP becomes very important in this process for two reasons. It provides a way to remember (anchor) how our body experiences that success as well as a strategy to bring back the desired feeling into our body (collapse anchors). This very basic form of collapsing the anchor of the resource state into the problem state can be accomplished with children's art by stating "when the negative feelings that go along with this problem picture come into your body, take a deep breath (to help relaxation and as a pattern interruption) and bring the feelings that go with the solution picture into your body."

As I continue to work with this chart, I find myself asking chil-dren what trait, quality, or attribute would they need to accom-plish this solution behavior. Their answers were often: self-control, patience, pride, and self-esteem. These traits help chil-dren access a feeling state they would need to help them accom-plish their solution behavior. Unfortunately, the words: trait, characteristic, quality, and attribute are not words with which children are familiar. Of the four components, the feeling compo-nent is often the most difficult for children to fully utilize. However, *children as young as six years old have been able to reduce anxiety by bringing the good feeling back into their bodies after attending only one therapy session.*

What is really important is that this is a mind body approach to behavior change. It is an approach that requires children to look deeper into themselves to find out what is going on below the surface behavior. The fact that children are successful in using this approach installs some very important strategies for personal growth throughout their lives.

Summary

This workbook will help children learn that there are ways that they reacted to problems in the past and that there are new ways to react to those same type of problems in the future. At one level, the workbook appears to offer a cookbook step-by-step approach to changing behavior. What is far more important is the deeper level of this workbook. The most impactful learning for some children may take place as a result of how the activities are processed by the parent, counselor, or guide who is working with children. *It is the guides job to point out to children that they are learning a process of change.* When the guide can cite other personal resources of the children and ways they have learned to change in the past, they are placed in a lifelong path of turning their problems into gifts.

Whatever your relationship is with the child you have worked with using this book, I am encouraging you to learn more about NLP for yourself and the child (or children) with which you are working. Like all other forms of mental imagery, we need to be respectful of its impact and the very literal way the subconscious mind responds to suggestions. If you are not a therapist, don't try to do therapy with imagery. If you are a therapist, make sure you have the training you need to do clean, elegant work. There are contraindications to using imagery with children and adults.

Please don't take imagery lightly. When you use imagery, you have dodged the conscious mind and have entered the subconscious world of the child. Learn what you need to know about children so that you can be respectful of their ecological needs. Remember that most negative behaviors resulted from a positive intention. It is important never to take away a behavior without making sure that there are no reservations at the subconscious level (ecology check). Before you ask children to take away a behavior, you should help them brainstorm for positive solutions that will replace the unwanted behavior.

In my work with children I use the chart "Understanding Your Behavior" to help children "chunk down" the process of perception. I have them interact with the chart in regard to each modality. The children can write down their self-talk in both the problem state and the solution state. They either describe or draw the pictures they make in their minds. In order to access the way their bodies experience a particular feeling, I request that they get themselves into a relaxed state and review the content of their self-talk and the submodalities of the pictures in their minds. After they identify the color of that feeling state, they color the box on the chart. That color becomes a visual anchor for them to re-access that state.

The final step is for the children to determine the way they will bring back the feeling state (now called a resource state) when it is needed. Some children will "coach themselves" (self-talk) to get it; others will see the picture. One client told me, "If you can't see it you can't be it." Other children can go directly to the place in their body that experiences the desired feeling state and bring that state back. When you ask children, they will be able to tell you which method will work best for them. Once they learn to bring the feeling back and use it when they need it, they gain a very essential feeling state-the feeling of being in control and empowered.

The methodology within this workbook can be a very potent tool for helping children with *Problems and Wishes*. It also can be fun. So enjoy the workbook, and most of all, enjoy the children with whom you are working.

Please remember: *You can be a very powerful personal resource for children!*

Happy anchoring!

Burt Wasserman

For Peer Leaders Only

Your Peer Leadership Program has chosen this workbook for you to use when you work with elementary school children. I suspect that they have chosen this workbook because people of all ages can use these strategies to make changes in their lives. So when you work with children to teach them concepts about themselves and how they can deal with stress and make changes in their lives, listen to your words because you can use them for yourself.

In your work with elementary school children, your goals have probably related to establishing a trusting relationship, and providing valuable information that the children can use to feel safe, cared for, and better about themselves. This workbook provides children with a different set of survival skills.

It helps children deal with stress and learn that they can make changes in the way they feel and the way they act. When children learn how to take control of their lives, they no longer feel helpless and powerless. Instead, they feel better about themselves.

This workbook teaches children to take control of their lives by teaching them how to turn their problems into gifts. The three steps to that process are to:

1. **See Things Differently**—Look at your problem in different ways and from different points of view.

2. **Discover New Meaning**—Look back and look ahead to find out what you have already learned or what you will learn when you get through this problem.

3. **Appreciate Yourself**—You have turned a problem into a gift. You have grown a little, gotten a little stronger or wiser, and probably feel a little better about yourself as a result of getting through a problem.

All the activities in this book relate to the three steps stated above. There are many different activities because we all have different learning styles. Some activities will work better for one child while another activity will fit best with a different child's learning style. Children are asked to draw their feelings and problems because it enables them to get those feelings out of their bodies and on to the paper. Some teenagers and adults still use the strategy of drawing their feelings to relieve their stress and see their problems differently. Others accomplish the same result by writing in journals or talking to someone. The important concept about using artwork for children is that it is one way to get the feelings out so you can start to see them differently.

You may choose to read the information for the other "guides" who might be counselors or parents working with children. If you do, you will learn that this workbook can be helpful for children who have problems learning in school. If you also have problems learning in school, you might want to show this book to a learning specialist in your school so that person might help you to improve the way you learn.

My hope is that you enjoy working with this book. I also encourage you to write me and tell me about your success. You might provide some valuable information that I could use in another book for children. *Don't forget to provide the name of your peer group and your school in your letter.*

About the Authors

Burt Wasserman is licensed by the Commonwealth of Virginia as a professional counselor and certified by the National Board for Certified Clinical Hypnotherapists. He holds an Educational Specialist degree from James Madison University and has been certified as a Master Practitioner of Neuro-Linguistic Programming. In addition to brief therapy, his specialty is working with children and their families.

Bill Coughlan is a graphic designer living in northern Virginia. He holds a Bachelor of Science degree in Computer Science from the College of William and Mary, and in addition to cartoon-style illustration, he works in multimedia on the Macintosh desktop computer, specializing in three-dimensional animation. He is currently working for a specialty consulting and publication firm based in Washington, D.C.

Bibliography

Armstrong-Brisson, Joan. (1988, September). "Using NLP in the elementary classroom." *Anchor Point*. Franktown, CO: Cahill Mountain Press. (800) 544-6480.

Bell, Nanci. (1986). *Visualizing and verbalizing*. Paso Robles, CA: Academy of Reading Publications. (800) 234-6224.

Grinder, Michael. (1991). *Righting the educational conveyor belt*. Portland, OR: Meta-morphous Press.

Jacobson, Sid. (1983-1986). *Meta-cation (I, II & III)*. Cupertino, CA: Meta Publications.

Lankton, Steve. *(1980). Practical magic—A translation of NLP into clinical psychotherapy*. Cupertino, CA: Meta Publications.

Lutzinger, Diane Famiano. (1990, February). "ADD and NLP." *Anchor Point*. Franktown, CO: Cahill Mountain Press. (800) 544-6480.

Mills, Joyce C. and Crowley, Richard. (1986). *Therapeutic metaphors for children and the child within*. New York: Brunner/Mazel.

Vitale, Barbara. (1982). *Unicorns are real: A right-brained approach to learning*. Rolling Hills Estates, CA: Jalmar Press.

Wasserman, Burt G. (1992, November). "Helping children change unwanted behaviors." *Anchor Point*. Franktown, CO: Cahill Mountain Press. (800) 544-6480.

Wasserman, Burt G. (1993, January). "Our mission in the 90's." *Anchor Point*. Franktown, CO: Cahill Mountain Press. (800) 544-6480.

Wasserman, Burt G. (1993, April). "Put it in the balloon." *Anchor Point*. Franktown, CO: Cahill Mountain Press. (800) 544-6480.

Wasserman, Burt G. (1993, July). "Integrating NLP with art therapy." *Anchor Point*. Franktown, CO: Cahill Mountain Press. (800) 544-6480.

Wasserman, Burt G. (1993, October). "Seven areas of beliefs and emotions." *Anchor Point*. Franktown, CO: Cahill Mountain Press. (800) 544-6480.

Wasserman, Burt G. (1994). Helping children deal with emotional pain. Unpublished.